Better Homes and Gardens®

Emma's Christmas Wish

A Child's Recipe for Love

by Sallyann J. Murphey
Illustrated by Cary Phillips

Produced by Meredith Custom Publishing,
1912 Grand Avenue, Des Moines, Iowa 50309-3379
Library of Congress Catalog Number: 96-75527
ISBN: 0-696-20612-9

Hallmark

*For Nandy Pat
and the generations
of women who
have kept
Christmas alive.*

4

Emma's Story

With their mother in the hospital, 13-year-old Emma and little sister Rosie are determined to make Mom well by keeping the family Christmas celebration and traditions alive. Can the family album, passed down for six generations, show them the way to make this Christmas wish come true?

47

Our Christmas Recipes

The Metcalfe family album is filled with recipes that have helped them celebrate the holidays for generations. Perhaps one of these recipes will become one of your family's favorites.

It began slowly—large puffs of white dropping lazily from a

pearl gray sky. In the fields, animals gathered silently in groups, seeking shelter
along the fence lines under the bare branches of the trees. They were the only
signs of life on an otherwise empty landscape. No voices carried on the early
morning air; no doors slammed; no cars came down the county road.
The world held its breath.

By ten o'clock, the storm had hit full force. Snow tumbled down, piling up
against gates and doorways, drifting across the drive and obliterating the road
beyond. It was a torrent of white, linking sky to earth and filling the old
farmhouse with bright, opalescent light.

Inside, all was quiet. The only sounds came from a clock ticking softly in the
well-scrubbed kitchen and the whisper of voices from somewhere upstairs.

"Rosie, please …this is our chance to find the stuff while Dad's away."

"But we're not allowed in the attic—it's dirty. There are cobwebs everywhere."

The owner of the first voice sighed. She was a slim, 13-year-old girl with bright green eyes and a mane of tawny curls, which seemed to fill the attic doorway as she blocked her small sister's retreat.

"Don't you want to have a good Christmas?" Emma wheedled. "How can we do that without all the Christmas stuff?"

"But Dad told us that we couldn't this year—no presents, no tree, no decorating, no carols, no cookies, no … anything …" Rosie's voice trailed off and her bottom lip began to quiver.

"That's not what he said," Emma corrected her gently. "What he said was that Mom won't be coming home."

The past few weeks had been very hard on both girls.

At the beginning of November their mother, Jan—the rock on whom the whole family depended—had become quite ill. Ten days before Thanksgiving, she'd been whisked off to a hospital a hundred miles away, for what their Dad had mysteriously called "tests." They hadn't seen her since.

"Rosie's not allowed to visit—she's too young," Dad had explained. "You'll have to be responsible for her, Emma, while your Mom's away." Their father was a man of few words and that's all they were told.

Then, last night, he had sat them down for a "serious talk."

"Girls," he began, "we'd better get used to the fact that your mother is very sick …" Emma's heart had started to pound—she could hear it in her ears drowning out her Dad's words, which only got through in snatches: "You have to be brave … Don't expect too much … I'm depending on you … Christmas impossible … Mom won't be home in time." They had listened mutely, then taken their tears to bed, unwilling to add to their father's obvious pain. Emma had tossed and turned—half-dreaming, half-awake—until just before dawn, when she sat up with a start. "That's it!" she whispered to herself, "That's what we have to do." The girl had then fallen into a deep sleep and was only awaken by the smell of breakfast drifting up the stairs.

"Listen, Rosie," she said now, gathering her sister onto her lap. "I had a dream last night and I think I know how to get Mom back."

The seven-year-old's dark eyes grew huge as she listened intently.

"I dreamed that we were having Christmas like always," Emma explained. "Except that Mom wasn't doing the work—it was you and me. We did everything just the way she likes it. Then, as we were hanging the Santa cookie up on Christmas Eve, we heard a voice saying what good children we'd been. It was her, Rosie. It was Mom—and she told us that our faith and hope had made her well. I have a feeling that if we can put a Christmas together, exactly the way she does it for us, Mom will be here to enjoy it."

The little girl nodded solemnly and got to her feet. "Okay. Where do we begin?"

It was a good question—one that had been worrying Emma all morning. The holidays were her mother's favorite time of year and she had their preparation down to a fine art. All Emma could remember was coming home from school one day to find the house magically transformed. The mechanics behind that operation were a mystery to her. "This is all new to me," she admitted to Rosie, "but getting the decorations out must be a good start."

The sisters weren't normally allowed in the attic because it was, simply, too full of stuff. Every available inch had been packed with all the abandoned bits and pieces that make up the history of an old home. Chipped sets of china leaned precariously against stacks of dusty boxes, and faded clothes lay piled on top of heaps of shoes. In one corner, a dressmaker's model stood festooned with hats, while in another, a one-eyed teddy bear took an everlasting ride on an ancient red tricycle.

The girls moved gingerly at first, ducking under cobwebs and stepping over the books that trailed across the floor. "Look!" Rosie shouted suddenly, swooping down on a crate full of wadded newspaper. "It's the ornament box!" Emma knelt down beside her and reached carefully into the paper packing.

Her hand closed on a small glass angel that had once been silver but was now a dull grey.

"We need some new decorations," Emma grumbled. "These are so old."

"They always look beautiful on the tree," Rosie reminded her. "They're my favorite part of Christmas."

"Are they?" Emma asked, considering for a moment. "I guess my favorite part is the smells. I remember noticing them last year when Mom was making gingerbread. The air was a wonderful mix of pine needles, oranges, baking cookies, and warm sugar..."

"...And don't forget Mom's perfume," Rosie added.

Emma smiled—the house was always filled with a faint whiff of it. The perfume was Mother's one self-indulgence—a hangover from her big-city beginnings as a single career woman in a business suit. These days, Jan Metcalfe dressed in sneakers and jeans, but she couldn't give up that daily dab of her former self.

"Can't you see her?" Emma mused quietly, "dancing across the kitchen between the table and the stove, mixing this and stirring that, then checking her recipe for the tenth time …"

"Her recipes …" Rosie echoed. "Recipes? Emma—what about our family book?"

Emma paused mid-daydream. It was there in her mind's eye: A battered leather scrapbook propped against the flour jar, the family record of all past festivities.

"Do you know where she keeps it?" Emma asked urgently.

"In the kitchen … I think …" Rosie hesitated.

Emma grabbed her sister's hand and they ran downstairs.

The Metcalfe family album had been started six generations before, when the girls' great-great-great-great-grandmother, Marianne, wrote her first recipe in the leather ledger she had brought with her from France. She did this in 1835, when the family was living in the log cabin that had once stood where the farmhouse stood today. The circumstances were a matter of record because Marianne had included a diary entry about her new home, after some instructions for Wheat Bread. Since then, all Metcalfe wives had taken their turn, contributing favorite recipes and crafts, and short paragraphs about their lives. Their mother had added to it often and, as the girls now discovered, kept the book in a kitchen drawer. They settled down to read it, passing over worn, yellowed pages and moving to the section where Grandma Jessie's precise script gave way to their Mom's distinctive scrawl. There was a recipe for Four Onion Soup and another for Mulled Wine, then Emma found what she'd hoped for—Jan's "Countdown to Christmas: A Guide to Holiday Plans."

"Here it is," she showed Rosie. "The perfect plan we can follow …"

Thirty miles away, their father was edging his way down the interstate.

A ribbon of red lights streamed ahead of him, as cars crawled through the snow,

slowing down even further to stare at jackknifed trucks. Their pace suited Ben

Metcalfe's mood. He was in no hurry to get home. In fact, if not for the girls, he

would have preferred to stay in the city, where he could be closer to his Jan.

She was the fire at which this quiet man warmed himself, the woman who had

breathed life into his various worlds. As the county veterinarian, Ben was famous

for treating animals in silence, dispensing prescriptions without uttering a word. It was his wife's charm that soothed patients and owners, and her organization that kept the office on track. They were the unlikely pair that makes a great team—his calm strength acting as anchor to Jan's optimism; her sparkle and laughter coaxing him out of his shell. At that moment, the prospect of returning to a house empty of his mate seemed so bleak that Ben pulled off the highway and headed in to his office.

However unwelcome, their father's absences did at least allow his two daughters to get on with their plans. The moment they finished school, they began working through their mother's list. Step One on Jan's countdown was to "give everything a thorough cleaning." The girls went at it with a will: washing walls, waxing floors, and polishing windows their grandma's way which, according to the album, was by using newspapers and white vinegar. In the evenings, they gravitated to the kitchen, where Rosie strung popcorn and cranberries while Emma read excerpts from the family book aloud.

"You're not going to believe this," she announced one night. "Wait 'til you hear what Great-great-grandma Anna has to say about her first Christmas at the farm:

"*December 1905—Anna Reich Metcalfe:*

This most important of holidays is a fearsome responsibility. They have so many family traditions and I am nervous of disappointing George. They must have Roast Turkey, he says, and his grandmother's Aioli for the Gros Souper on Christmas Eve. He wants me to make her spice cake (although, in my opinion, the German gingerbread is better), and his mother's Speculaas, or little Dutch cookies.

He shall have it all—but I will also introduce some customs of my own.

This year, the Metcalfes will taste Lebkuchen (my homeland's honey cakes) and Christollen, that most sacred Christmas bread. And we will have a Tannenbaum, decorated with the ornaments that we brought from Germany. I will tell little Theodore about my village, where some of the finest glass decorations are blown, and I will show him the little angel that my father made for me …"

Rosie gasped. "You don't think …?"

"I do," Emma admitted ruefully. "And it will have a special place on our tree."

"Where are we going to get a Christmas tree?"

"Well, if we can't persuade Dad to buy one," Emma said, "we can copy Great-grandma Kathleen's idea during the Depression. Listen …

"*Christmas 1933—Kathleen O'Loughlin Metcalfe:*

This has been a hard year. There's no work and the children languish at home because the school is closed. Life's as poor as it was in Ireland—I never thought to see Americans going without shoes. Men have come to our door for food, but we've had precious little to share, living as we do on potatoes and beans, and all the rabbits that Teddy can shoot. This family needs a good Christmas—but how to manage it? There's no money to spend and I bartered our last turkey to pay that doctor's bill. We could spare a chicken, I suppose, and we do have onions and apples a-plenty. I can make that Four Onion Soup of my mam's and bake some deep-dish pies. At least we're not short of flour or fat—and the Christmas greening will be free. The children can pick as much holly and ivy as they please and I'll cut down some fir branches to form into a tree …"

"That sounds terrible!" Rosie protested.

"It may be all we have," Emma reasoned, "and that's better than nothing at all."

"I s'pose." Her sister sounded unconvinced. "By the way, can we make some of that soup?"

"Of course!" Emma exclaimed. "Christmas Eve wouldn't be the same without it."

The girls had been putting together their Christmas menus, using Jan's guide. Some dishes were decided for them generations ago, when they were written into family lore. Grandma Jessie's Roast Beef and Yorkshire Pudding, for instance, was always the main course at Christmas dinner, while Christmas Eve supper was traditionally a buffet, where the family could pick at a variety of foods while they went about their final preparations—which included hanging the large Dutch cookie of Saint Nicholas that had been baked as an offering to Santa Claus every year since 1870. Mince pies and plum pudding had been standard desserts since the second World War, and little crocks of *Rumtopf* (summer fruits preserved in liquor) had been prepared as gifts for unexpected guests for almost a century. The other choices were up to the cook of the day, and some heavy negotiating went into the sisters' final list.

"I want macaroons, vanilla fudge, marzipan, Turkish Delight, coconut ice, and peppermint creams," Rosie declared. "And we must make sugar cookies, shortbread, peanut brittle, vanilla crescents, lemon curd tarts, and Nana Jessie's Battenberg cake."

"Rosie, that would take months! We've only got three weeks," Emma reminded her. "And don't forget, we have to leave time for the gingerbread village."

"You're not going to try *that?*" Rosie was incredulous.

"Why not?" Emma shrugged. "Mom makes one every year."

Although Emma had encouraged Rosie to be creative, she had also been careful to keep to her mother's plan. Jan's gingerbread village was the annual centerpiece on her spectacular Christmas table. If they didn't attempt it, Emma feared, the magic in her dream wouldn't work.

"All right," Rosie said reluctantly. "I'll cut my list down—but we're gonna make some candies and that Battenberg cake."

For the next few days, the old kitchen came alive with sounds of clinking bowls, crashing pans, and bursts of helpless giggles. Emma was a good cook, as Jan had taught her well (and she had won a fistful of ribbons at the county fair), but the girls still had their share of disasters. Pastry burned, sponge cake sank, and the Christollen bread almost blew the oven door off.

"Watch out!" Rosie shrieked. "It's going to explode." Both girls stared at the gigantic balloon of dough that hissed and heaved against the oven window. Emma scratched her head. "I don't understand. I followed all the instructions." She went over to the book and checked the recipe again. "See … exactly as it says."

"Not quite," Rosie pointed out, peering over her shoulder. "You were supposed to split it into six loaves!"

The girls cleaned up carefully after each session, storing their goods at the back of the pantry.

"Why don't we show Dad what we're doing?" Rosie asked.

"I'm not trying to deceive him," Emma explained. "He's bound to know soon. I'm just afraid that he'll stop us if he finds out now."

She needn't have worried. Throughout it all, Ben came and went, too tired to notice strange fragrances or the odd sprinkling of flour. The man was exhausted. His constant anxiety about Jan wore away at him, until each day felt like a new mountain to climb. The doctors had finally discovered what was wrong. Hanta virus, they called it, an illness that was new to America—but they had no medicines to offer. His wife's body had to fight this off alone, they said, and all Ben could do was watch, increasingly consumed by his own frustration.

The girls finished their cooking ten days before Christmas and decided it was time to decorate the house.

"Dad's bound to realize now," Rosie said anxiously.

"That's okay," Emma assured her. "It might even do him good."

They started, as always, with the Christmas bird tree—a small potted pine that was strung with berries, seeds, and little balls of suet, then set out on the back porch where their feathered friends could be observed from the dining room window. Ben even brushed by it in the dark, but he didn't discover the girls' secret until the following afternoon, when he came home early to find them draping garland on the stairs.

"What are you two up to?" he asked, mildly amused.

Rosie looked guilty and Emma looked resigned.

"Dad, I know what you said," she began, "but we thought we should go ahead with Christmas anyway in case Mom's home in time. You know how disappointed she'd be if the house wasn't just so, and we've done most of the work already. We haven't made a mess."

"I can see that," he nodded, then glanced around, taking in all the details. The windows glittered, the floors shone, and there wasn't a speck of dust anywhere to be seen. A freshly made holly wreath hung above the mantelpiece, where the family's silver tea set stood, freshly polished, just the way it had on every holiday since Ben was a boy. "You've been busy," he murmured.

"And that's not all," Rosie burst out, "we've made the Christmas food as well." She took him by the hand and led him to the kitchen, where Emma silently opened the pantry door. Her father stood there, speechless. Across the countertop and along the shelves were boxes and baskets, jars and plates, all filled with seasonal goodies. The sisters had outdone themselves, making everything on Rosie's list and then some. There were cookies and candies, plates of fudge, and carefully wrapped cakes—and in the center of it all, a wobbly gingerbread village that lovingly echoed their mother's design. Ben reached out and touched a lopsided roof. His eyes were damp.

"You must have worked very hard," he said in a strangled voice.

"Just wait 'til you see the freezer," Emma replied.

A teasing smile flashed across her face and Ben's heart lurched: She was so like her mom. Those endless days he'd spent missing Jan and she'd been here all the time, living through these beautiful girls. He had assumed that he was being the strong one, shouldering this situation all on his own, but now he realized that it was the children who had shown the true courage by never giving up hope.

"I have been a fool," Ben whispered, beckoning to his daughters with both arms open wide.

Christmas, 1963—Jessie Maynard Metcalfe:

"I hadn't planned to do much this year—with Patrick gone, I didn't really feel like it—but a little miracle happened yesterday that has completely changed my mind. Ben, who's been disturbingly quiet for weeks, came to me for our first talk together since his father died.

"Mom, I don't want to push," he said, "but we must have Christmas. Dad would want us to and the twins deserve all the fun that I had when I was small."

He sounded so much older than his twelve years. He was quite the little man.

"You won't have to do all the work," he promised me. "I'll do my share."

True to his word, he began this morning: splitting wood and hauling greenery and stringing lights around the yard. Then this afternoon, he scared me half to death by disappearing for three hours. He turned up again just before dark, in the back of Mr. Walker's truck. Apparently, he'd ridden his bicycle into the village to persuade the old man to bring us up a tree. Walker grumbled that he had tried to refuse at first because the roads were so bad— 'but that son o' yourn wouldn't take no for an answer.' He is a boy transformed."

"Em'! Rosie! Get down here!" Their father sounded excited. Emma slid the packages they had been wrapping back under her bed and the girls ran downstairs. "I've got a surprise for you," Ben announced. "I want you both to close your eyes and come into the living room." He led them in, then told them they could look. In front of them, already standing in its traditional corner, was the tallest, straightest, bushiest blue spruce that either of them had ever seen. It was their turn to be speechless. "Do you like it?" Ben asked timidly.

"It's beautiful!" Rosie replied, without taking her eyes off the tree. "It's the most wonderful tree in the world."

"Well, don't just stand there," Ben said, sounding gratified. "Let's get decorating."

The first ornament to go up was the little angel, which Emma hung at eye level

for everyone to see. Then they turned to the rest of the collection, greeting each new decoration like a long-lost friend:

"Look, Rosie! Your baby cradle ..."

"Here's Mom's little wooden spoons ..."

"Well, I'll be ... It's my old bicycle ..."

Ben stood with the tiny battered model in his hand.

"Your grandmother gave me this," he mused, "to commemorate a very special Christmas."

As they worked, Ben reported on his morning's visit to the hospital.

"I told your Mom all about your recent efforts and she spoke for the first time in days."

"She did!" Emma exclaimed. "What did she say?"

"Good children …" Ben reached up to fill in a blank spot near the top. "She said what good children you've been," he went on "which is true." He turned away too quickly to notice the shocked look in Emma's eyes. "I was thinking that, if she continues to improve, the hospital might let you both visit after the holidays." This time, he caught his daughter's disappointed expression.

"Em' … " he said softly. "We're lucky to have come this far. Don't worry, the three of us can still have a wonderful time."

Emma shook herself. "Yes, I know we can," she agreed. "Now, would anyone like some hot chocolate, while we finish the tree?"

"Good idea!" Ben nodded approvingly, pleased with Emma's level-headedness.

"I'll go and make some, then."

Her father would not have been so happy if he'd seen the stubborn determination on his daughter's face as she stomped out to the kitchen.

Ben wasn't even suspicious when Emma came to him the following week with the monumental list of groceries she wanted for the holiday meals.

"This is rather a lot," he commented.

"It's for several days!"

"I realize that, but do we really need a rib roast for just the three of us?"

"Dad, we always have roast beef at Christmas," Emma said firmly. "By the way, are you going to the hospital on Christmas Eve?"

"I thought I should. I won't be there on Christmas Day, after all. Why?"

"Well, I was hoping that you'd have time for a small celebration before you leave," she explained.

"That's not a problem," he said, intrigued. "I wasn't planning to drive up until later, anyway."

"Good!" Emma looked pleased. "Just one more thing: Do you have anything to do that might take you out of the house that afternoon?" Ben's eyes twinkled.

"I could probably find something. What time am I expected home?" he inquired.

"Oh, about five o'clock would be fine," she replied airily, disappearing before he could ask any more questions.

At exactly 5:00 p.m. on Christmas Eve, Ben Metcalfe

found himself knocking at his own front door. He had a key, of course, but presumed that he was the guest of honor at a special event and should

announce his arrival. Emma let him in—not as the tousled-haired teenager he'd seen flying around the kitchen that morning, but a young lady, dressed in a skirt and embroidered sweater, with her tawny curls piled carefully on top of her head. Her little sister stood behind her, shiny as a new penny, in the tartan dress that Jan had made for her that fall.

"Well, look at you two," Ben said appreciatively.

"There's a clean shirt on your bed," Emma announced, "and fresh towels in your bathroom."

"Apparently, I have my marching orders," he observed, heading up the stairs. "I'll be down in a few minutes."

His room had been prepared. A fire burned in the grate and, as promised, his freshly ironed shirt was laid out on the pillow. On his bedside table stood a steaming glass of something, which Ben quickly identified as his favorite Christmas treat—mulled cider. "How did she know that?" he wondered. "Curioser and curioser …"

He was going to ask her when he came back down, but his daughter pre-empted him.

"Time to eat," she declared. The three of them walked across the big hall to the dining room, whose double doors were tightly shut. The girls positioned themselves by each one, then ceremoniously threw them open.

Inside, the room was bathed in light. There were candles everywhere—in the windows, along the mantelpiece, and lined up on the table. Their reflections leaped and flickered in the gleaming wood, bouncing off silverware and making the crystal sparkle.

"Girls, this is beautiful," their father gasped.

"Why don't we sit down?" Emma suggested.

Ben pulled out his chair, then stopped to survey the array of food in front of him. He couldn't contain his curiosity for another second.

"Em', how have you managed all this?" he blurted out. "You can't have learned all these recipes and traditions just by watching your mother?"

"Of course not!" she laughed. "I didn't have to. Everything's written down in the family album."

Ben looked blank for a moment. "Oh! The old scrapbook, you mean?" His face cleared. "I'd forgotten all about that. I haven't looked at it since I was a child."

"Mom has," Emma went on. "She adds to it often. We used her 'Countdown to Christmas' as our guide, then branched out and tried some of the other recipes. In fact, there's a dish here from every woman in the family."

"Show me," Ben said, looking around.

"The wheat bread is from Great-great-great-great-grandma Marianne," said Emma. "She started the book, you know, in 1835, on the way up here from Louisville. The *Harringsla'* is Great-great-great-grandma Constance's recipe—it's Dutch, just like she was. The onion soup comes from Great-grandma Kathleen's kitchen, and the potatoes are Mom's idea. Mom made Great-great-grandma Anna's *Rumtopf* for dessert, or you can have Nana Jessie's favorite: lemon curd tarts."

"You talk about them all as if you know them," Ben remarked.

"I feel like I do," said Emma. "They've each told their stories from the things they wrote. None of this Christmas would have been possible without their help."

For a moment, it felt as though there were five shadowy figures around them, smiling down at the table. Ben could almost see the striking French woman from all those years ago, with her dark hair tucked inside a mob cap, or his mother, as he remembered her from boyhood: wasp-waisted, wearing full-flowing skirts. He rubbed his eyes.

"So what kinds of things does your Mom write about?" he asked.

"Lots of stuff!" Rosie declared. "Want to hear some?"

Emma fetched the album. "Here's one of my favorite bits," she said, thumbing through the pages. "Mom's thoughts on the meaning of Christmas:

"Christmas 1989—Jan Andersen Metcalfe:

We had a couple of "firsts" this year: Rosie's first Christmas and the first time that Emma's been big enough to help. As usual, between the two of them, my daughters have made me think.

Rosie started it when she pushed aside the toy we'd given her and played with the box instead! As I watched, I realized how often I'd done the same thing. How many times have I obsessed so much about the wrappings of the holidays that I've forgotten the gift inside?

Real Christmas cheer can't be found in the trappings and trimmings, gifts, or good food. When we truly search for the joys of this season, we find them in our children. My daughters' innocent pleasure helps me to rediscover some innocence of my own—while their immense capacity for love allows me to believe, however briefly, that the world can improve, that we will do better and that, maybe, these little girls could learn to keep Christmas all the year.

It's a dream that I share with Jessie and Kathleen and every woman in this family book.

It binds us together across the centuries and has fueled each generation's need to observe this celebration. Without it, hanging the holly or baking Christmas cakes would be empty gestures. With it, these things become symbols of the continuity of life.

As I taught Emma how to green the house and make the cookies this year, I imagined her ancestors learning those same lessons. And I understood that when my daughter teaches these traditions in her turn, she will carry each woman's love, laughter, wishes, and hopes into the future—while keeping our past very much alive."

Emma quietly closed the album.

"I'm not sure I understand," Rosie piped up.

"You will," Ben murmured, "because you're lucky enough to have a Mom and a sister who can explain. I'm very proud of you, Em'."

His daughter blushed. "You know, we really should begin before everything gets cold," she said, changing the subject.

"At last!" Rosie exclaimed. "I'm starved."

By the time the meal was finished, Rosie was sleepy as well, so Ben took her up to bed before he got ready to leave. Emma headed for the kitchen.

"I'm going to be home very late," Ben said, stopping by the door. "So don't wait for me." He came over to kiss his daughter. "And get to bed early. You've been working too hard."

She leaned into him. "I've got one more thing to do, then I'll go right up," she promised.

Once Ben had left, Emma sat down at the kitchen table and opened the album for one last time before Christmas. The final entry on Jan's countdown read: "Prepare sweet rolls for baking in the morning."

Emma couldn't imagine a Christmas that didn't begin with this delicious breakfast and she was looking forward to completing the last task on her list. "Then I'll have done it all," she thought proudly, "and Mom will be coming home." She flicked through the pages of Jan's section, searching for the recipe. When she came to the spot where her mother's writing stopped, she went back and looked more carefully. The recipe wasn't there. "It must be earlier on," Emma concluded and began to scan the entire book. A lump was forming in her throat. The pages turned and turned, but still it wasn't there. Emma's hands began to shake. There were no sweet rolls to be found.

"Maybe she kept it somewhere else," Emma hoped out loud, moving over to the shelf where her mother's cookbooks stood. There was nothing—no book about baking, no hidden card, not even a recipe for homemade bread. In her heart, Emma knew that if Jan had written it down anywhere, it would have been in the family album and could only guess that this was one occasion when her mother carried both ingredients and method in her head. She slumped down on her chair, utterly defeated.

It was late, she was tired, and now she knew that she had failed.

"Who was I kidding?" she said bitterly. "It was only a stupid dream."

Emma dragged herself upstairs, where she cried herself to sleep.

The sunshine that came streaming through her window the following morning felt like a bad joke. The teenager buried her head in the pillow and didn't stir until Ben came into her room. "Merry Christmas, sweetheart!" he declared. "Come and have some breakfast."

Emma reluctantly complied, knowing already what a disappointment the day would be. She put her robe on and slowly made her way downstairs.

As her foot hit the bottom step, Emma stopped. What was that smell—that sweet medley of cinnamon and fresh yeast? Could it be …? She ran into the living room. There, sitting on the coffee table, which had been placed by the tree, were cups and jugs, and a large plate of Christmas sweet rolls. Emma pointed at them.

"How did you …?" She sounded outraged.

Ben was smiling—no, grinning—for the first time in weeks.

"I've always made the breakfast," he explained. "It was the one Christmas job that your mom would let me do."

"Only because he wouldn't give me the recipe," said a soft voice from behind her.

Emma stood still and almost didn't dare to look. She turned slowly to find a pale but upright Jan, standing by the door.

For a moment, nobody moved, then Jan held her arms out. "Merry Christmas, my girls."

Emma and Rosie flung themselves at her.

"You made me well," their mom whispered, between kisses and tears.

Eventually, she led them back to the tree, where Ben stood with an envelope, adorned with ribbon and Emma's name written on the front. He gave it to her.

"After all you've done, Em', I thought that you should be the one to record the sweet roll recipe in the family book."

His daughter beamed at him and he moved forward to join them all in another hug.

As the four sets of arms went around each other, Emma closed her eyes. She drank in the fragrance of pine, warm sugar, wood smoke, and spices—and finally, that faint whiff of Mom's perfume.

The End

Our Christmas Recipes

*M*any a Christmas memory and tradition revolves around the holiday kitchen. For the Metcalfe family, the warm, inviting smells of savory meals and colorful sweets filled their home with love and the spirit of the Christmas holidays. With favorite recipes, passed down from generation to generation, the family bond became ever stronger.

Enjoy these recipes and share them with your family for a Christmas to remember!

Christmas Morning Cinnamon Rolls

As a gift of time for the elf in charge of Christmas breakfast, make and shape these rolls the day before, then chill in the refrigerator.

3½ to 4 cups all-purpose flour		2	Tbsp. margarine or butter, softened
1	pkg. active dry yeast	¾	cup packed brown sugar
1	cup milk	2	tsp. ground cinnamon
⅓	cup margarine or butter	½	cup raisins
⅓	cup sugar	½	cup chopped nuts
½	tsp. salt	4	tsp. half-and-half or light cream
1	egg		

In a large mixing bowl stir together 1½ cups of the flour and the yeast; set aside. In a small saucepan heat milk, ⅓ cup margarine or butter, sugar, and salt till warm (120° to 130°) and margarine or butter is almost melted. Add to flour mixture. Add egg. Beat with an electric mixer on low speed for 30 seconds, scraping bowl constantly. Beat on high speed for 3 minutes. Using a wooden spoon, stir in as much of the remaining flour as you can.

Turn dough out onto a lightly floured surface. Knead in enough remaining flour to make a moderately soft dough that is smooth and elastic (3 to 5 minutes total). Shape dough into a ball. Place dough in a lightly greased bowl; turn once. Cover; let rise in a warm place till double (1 to 1½ hours).

Punch dough down. Turn dough onto a lightly floured surface. Cover and let rest for 10 minutes. Roll dough into an 18x10-inch rectangle. Spread with softened margarine or butter. Combine brown sugar and cinnamon; sprinkle onto dough. Sprinkle with raisins and nuts.

Tightly roll up, jelly-roll style, starting from one of the long sides. Pinch seams to seal. Cut dough crosswise into 12 slices. Arrange slices, cut sides down, in a greased 13x9x2-inch baking pan. Cover and let rise till nearly double (about 30 to 40 minutes).

Or, cover with oiled waxed paper, then with plastic wrap. Chill in the refrigerator for 2 to 24 hours. To bake, let stand for 20 minutes at room temperature. Uncover and puncture any surface bubbles with a greased wooden toothpick.

Brush dough with half-and-half or light cream. Bake in a 350° oven for 25 to 30 minutes or till golden. Invert rolls onto a wire rack or serving platter. Cool slightly. Makes 12.

Masterpiece Beef Roast

God rest ye merry, gentlemen! With savory roast beef on the table (and maybe Yorkshire pudding), merriment's almost assured.

- 1 4- to 6-lb. beef rib roast
- 2 Tbsp. olive oil
- 1 Tbsp. dried minced onion
- 2 tsp. bottled minced garlic

Cut 1-inch-deep pockets on fat side of roast at 3-inch intervals. If desired, sprinkle roast with salt and pepper. In a small bowl combine olive oil, onion, and garlic. Rub mixture onto roast and into pockets.

Place meat, fat side up, in a 15½x10½x2-inch roasting pan. Insert a meat thermometer into the thickest portion of meat without touching fat or bone. Roast in a 325° oven for 1¾ to 2 hours for medium-rare (145°), 2¼ to 2½ hours for medium (155°), or 2¾ to 3 hours for well done (165°). (Temperature will rise 5° on standing.)

Transfer to serving platter; cover with foil. Let stand for at least 15 minutes before carving. Turn oven temperature to 450° if preparing Yorkshire pudding, see recipe, below). Makes 10 to 12 main-dish servings.

Pepper-Cheddar Yorkshire Pudding

In Britain, Christmas is not Christmas without roast beef, and beef is not beef without a savory Yorkshire pudding served at its side.

- Pan drippings from a 4- to 6- lb. beef rib roast
- 4 eggs
- 2 cups milk
- 1¾ cups all-purpose flour
- ¼ tsp. pepper
- ¼ tsp. salt
- 2 oz. extra-sharp cheddar cheese, finely shredded (½ cup)

After removing the roast from the oven, measure pan drippings. If necessary, add cooking oil to drippings to make ¼ cup; divide drippings and pour into two 8x8x2-inch or 9x9x2-inch square pans. Place pans in a 450° oven for 2 minutes or till slightly hot.

In a mixing bowl combine eggs and milk. Add flour, pepper, and salt. Beat with a rotary beater or whisk till smooth. Divide egg mixture evenly between the pans; stir into drippings in pans. Bake in the 450° oven about 25 minutes or till puffed and brown. Sprinkle with cheese. Cut into squares; serve at once with roast. Makes 8 to 10 side-dish servings.

Piquant Potatoes

Less is more: Lemon and chives are all it takes to turn simple potatoes into splendid eating.

2	lb. new potatoes (about 16), halved	1	Tbsp. lemon juice
2	Tbsp. margarine or butter		Few dashes white pepper or black pepper
1	tsp. finely shredded lemon peel	2	Tbsp. snipped fresh chives

In a large saucepan cook potatoes in boiling water, covered, for 10 to 12 minutes or just till tender; drain in a colander. Add margarine or butter to saucepan; heat and stir till melted. Remove from heat. Stir in lemon peel, juice, and pepper; add potatoes and toss gently to coat. Turn into a serving bowl. Sprinkle with chives. Makes 8 side-dish servings.

Savory Sprouts and Apples

Brussels sprouts become holiday fare when spruced up with spicy mustard and sweet apples; Jonathans or Rome Beauties make a good choice.

- 4 cups fresh brussels sprouts (about 1 lb.) or two 10-oz. pkg. frozen brussels sprouts
- 1 medium onion, finely chopped (½ cup)
- 1 Tbsp. margarine or butter
- ⅓ cup apple cider or apple juice
- 2 Tbsp. Dijon-style or coarse-grain brown mustard
- ¼ tsp. salt
- ⅛ tsp. pepper
- 2 small apples, unpeeled, cored, and thinly sliced

Halve any large sprouts. In a large saucepan cook fresh brussels sprouts, covered, in boiling, lightly salted water over medium heat about 10 minutes or till just tender. (Or, cook frozen sprouts according to package directions.) Drain; return to saucepan to keep warm.

Meanwhile, in a medium skillet cook onion in hot margarine or butter over medium heat about 5 minutes or till tender. In a small bowl stir together apple cider or apple juice, mustard, salt, and pepper; stir into onion mixture. Add apple slices; cook, uncovered, for 2 to 3 minutes more or till apple is crisp-tender, stirring gently once or twice.

Add onion-apple mixture to brussels sprouts in saucepan; toss gently to coat. Transfer to a serving dish. Makes 8 side-dish servings.

Mulled Cider

Cardamom, allspice, and cinnamon smell like Christmas-in-the-making.

8	cups apple cider or apple juice	1	tsp. whole allspice
2	to 4 Tbsp. packed brown sugar		Cinnamon sticks (optional)
		2	cardamom pods, cracked (about ½ tsp. seed)

In a large saucepan combine apple cider or juice and brown sugar. For the spice bag, cut a double thickness of 100 percent cotton cheesecloth into a 6- or 8-inch square. Place cardamom seeds and whole allspice in the center. Bring up corners; tie with a clean string. Add to cider mixture. Bring to boiling; reduce heat. Cover and simmer for at least 10 minutes. Discard spice bag. To serve, pour into a large punch bowl or mugs. If desired, garnish with cinnamon sticks. Makes 8 (8-ounce) servings.

Mulled Wine

Sugar and spice and everything nice go into this soul-warming sipper.

1½   cups water
½   cup sugar
2   oranges, sliced
10   whole cloves

2   4-inch sticks cinnamon
1   750 ml. bottle dry red wine*
¼   cup brandy

In a large saucepan combine water, sugar, and half of the orange slices. To make a spice bag, cut a double thickness of 100 percent cotton cheesecloth into a 6- or 8-inch square. Place cloves and stick cinnamon in center of cloth. Bring up corners and tie together with a clean string. (Or, place cloves in a tea strainer.) Add spices to the mixture in the saucepan.

Bring to boiling; reduce heat. Simmer, uncovered, for 10 minutes. Remove and discard orange slices and spices. Add wine and brandy. Cook, uncovered, over medium heat till heated through. (Do not allow to boil). To serve, pour into a large punch bowl or mugs. Garnish with additional orange slices. Makes about 8 (4-ounce) servings.

Tip: It is not necessary (nor wise!) to use expensive wine for this recipe. Any burgundy-type will do.

Dill Wheat Bread

Emma and Rosie, who gained their baking prowess by helping in the kitchen, made this bread without their mother's help. Your own children can lend a hand in shaping these loaves into wreaths.

2¾   to 3¼ cups all-purpose flour
1   pkg. active dry yeast
2   tsp. dried dillweed
¼   tsp. pepper
1¾   cups water

3   Tbsp. margarine or butter
2   Tbsp. packed brown sugar
1½   tsp. salt
2   cups whole wheat flour
Milk

In a large mixing bowl combine 2 cups of the all-purpose flour, the yeast, dillweed, and pepper; set aside. In a medium saucepan heat and stir water, margarine or butter, brown sugar, and salt till warm (120° to 130°) and margarine or butter is almost melted. Add to flour mixture and beat with an electric mixer on low to medium speed for 30 seconds, scraping bowl. Beat on high speed for 3 minutes. Using a wooden spoon, stir in whole wheat flour and as much of the remaining all-purpose flour as you can.

Turn dough onto a lightly floured surface. Knead in enough of the remaining all-purpose flour to make a moderately stiff dough that is smooth and elastic (6 to 8 minutes total). Shape into a ball. Place in a lightly greased bowl, turning dough once to grease surface. Cover and let rise in a warm place till double in size (about 60 minutes).

Punch dough down. Turn out onto a lightly floured surface. Divide dough in half. Shape each half into a ball. Cover and let rest for 10 minutes. Meanwhile, grease 2 baking sheets.

With floured fingers, make a hole in the center of each ball of dough. Stretch dough to form a circle about 8 inches in diameter, with an opening in the center about 4 inches across. Place circles on prepared baking sheets.

Using kitchen scissors, cut slits diagonally from outside about two-thirds of the way to the center of each circle of dough at about 1¼-inch intervals. Stretch center again, if necessary, to maintain the 4-inch opening. Cover and let rise in a warm place till nearly double (about 30 to 45 minutes).

Bake in a 350° oven for 25 to 30 minutes or till bread sounds hollow when tapped with fingers. Immediately brush tops of loaves with milk. Transfer bread to wire racks to cool. Makes 2 loaves (32 servings).

Four-Onion Soup

In case you're counting, it's the intriguing combination of leeks, onions, garlic, and chives that flavors the pot. By purée-ing the blend, we've created a creamy texture that also makes this onion soup distinctive.

¼ cup margarine or butter
3 cups thinly sliced leeks (white part only)
6 medium onions, halved and thinly sliced
   (4½ cups)
2 Tbsp. minced garlic (12 cloves)
1 Tbsp. sugar
6 cups chicken broth
1 tsp. dried thyme, crushed

¼ tsp. pepper
2 Tbsp. all-purpose flour
2 slightly beaten egg yolks
¼ cup Marsala wine or sweet sherry (optional)
1 cup half-and-half or light cream
Baguette-style French bread slices, toasted
Fresh chives (optional)
Fresh thyme (optional)

In a large pot melt margarine or butter. Stir in leeks, onions, garlic, and sugar. Cook, covered, over medium-low heat about 10 minutes or till tender, stirring occasionally. Remove ¾ cup onion mixture; set aside. Add 5½ cups of the chicken broth, the thyme, and pepper to remaining mixture in pan. Bring to boiling; reduce heat. Simmer, covered, over low heat for 20 minutes.

Remove from heat; cool slightly. Transfer one-third of the mixture to a blender container or food processor bowl. Cover and blend or process mixture till smooth. Repeat with remaining mixture. Return all of the pureed mixture to the pot.

In a small bowl stir together the remaining ½ cup chicken broth and flour till smooth. Stir in egg yolks. Gradually add 1 cup of the hot soup to egg mixture; stir mixture into remaining soup. Cook and stir over medium-high heat till thickened and bubbly. Add Marsala or sherry, if desired, and reserved onion-leek mixture. Cook and stir for 1 minute more; reduce heat. Stir in half-and-half or light cream.* Cook and stir till heated through; do not boil.

To serve, ladle into a large soup tureen or individual bowls. Top each serving with a toasted baguette slice. Sprinkle with chives and thyme, if desired. Makes 10 cups (6 main-dish servings).

*Make-ahead directions: Cover and refrigerate soup for up to 24 hours. At serving time, cook and stir till heated through; do not boil.

Herring Salad (Harringsla')

Dutch fanciers of herring devour the fresh fish with gusto throughout summer. But in the cold days that follow, herring pickled in vinegar and spices is used to make this hearty salad.

2 medium red-skinned potatoes
¼ cup light mayonnaise or salad dressing
4 tsp. sweet pickle juice
   Lettuce leaves
2 cups pickled herring
4 small sweet pickles (gherkins), sliced

½ of a small red onion, thinly sliced
1 16-oz. can sliced beets, chilled, drained
   and cut into strips
   Fresh dill sprigs (optional)

In a saucepan cook unpeeled potatoes, covered, in boiling salted water for 20 to 25 minutes or till just tender. Drain and cool. Carefully cut into slices; cover and chill. For dressing, in a small bowl stir together mayonnaise or salad dressing and pickle juice; cover and chill.

In a large bowl or individual salad bowls lined with lettuce leaves, arrange herring, pickles, and onion; cover and chill. At serving time, arrange potatoes and beets atop the herring mixture. Serve with dressing. If desired, garnish with dill. Makes 6 side-dish servings.

Macaroons

A chocolate drizzle brings these dainty coconut cookies up to dress code for the holiday cookie platter.

- 3 egg whites
- 1 cup sugar
- 2 cups flaked coconut (about 5 oz.)
- 1 oz. semisweet chocolate
- 2 tsp. shortening

In a large mixing bowl beat egg whites with an electric mixer on high speed till soft peaks form (tips curl). Gradually add sugar, a tablespoon at a time, beating till stiff peaks form (tips stand straight). Fold in coconut. Drop by rounded teaspoons 2 inches apart onto a greased cookie sheet. Bake in a 325° oven about 20 minutes or till edges of cookies are light brown. Cool cookies on a wire rack. Store in an airtight container.

To serve, in a small saucepan heat and stir chocolate and shortening over low heat till melted and smooth. Cool slightly. Transfer chocolate mixture to a heavy self-sealing plastic bag; seal. Cut a small hole in one corner of bag; use hole to pipe chocolate over cookies. Let stand till chocolate is set. Makes about 45 cookies.

Clockwise from far left,
Cranberry Shortbread, Peppermint Creams, Vanilla Nut Crescents, Favorite Sugar Cookies, Speculaas, Macaroons, Turkish Delight, Vanilla Fudge, and Lebkuchen

Turkish Delight

...and a favorite English Christmas treat. The Turkish name for this candy means "rest for the throat," which couldn't be more timely during December's dining orgies. Kids love the way it jiggles.

1½	cups sugar		1	tsp. strawberry flavoring or ¾ tsp. rose water*
3	envelopes unflavored gelatin		1	to 2 drops red food coloring
¾	cup cold water		⅔	cup sifted powdered sugar
1	tsp. lemon juice			

In a 1-quart saucepan combine the 1½ cups sugar and gelatin; add water and lemon juice. Cook and stir over low heat till dissolved. Remove from heat. Add strawberry flavoring or rose water; tint mixture pink with food coloring. Cool to room temperature.

Pour mixture into a greased 8x4x2-inch loaf pan. Cover and chill 2 hours or overnight or till firm. Sift some powdered sugar onto a sheet of waxed paper. Loosen edges of candy with a knife; invert pan onto the sifted sugar. (If the candy does not easily separate from the pan, dip pan for just a few seconds into a larger pan of warm water, then invert.)

Cut candy into 24 to 32 bite-size pieces. Turn to coat all sides with powdered sugar. Place each piece in a paper candy cup. Store, refrigerated, in an airtight container for up to 1 week. Toss candy in additional powdered sugar before serving, if necessary. Makes 24 to 32 pieces.

Note: You can find rose water in health-food stores and Middle-Eastern specialty shops.

Vanilla Fudge

The Better Homes and Gardens® Test Kitchen taste panel gave it a Ten: "creamy," "smooth," and with "lots of vanilla flavor," it's a pleasant change from the chocolate classic. Because it needs to be beaten the old-fashioned way, the more helping hands on deck, the better!

2	cups sugar		¼	cup butter
1	5-oz. can (⅔ cup) evaporated milk		1	tsp. vanilla
⅓	cup milk			Broken nuts (optional)
⅛	tsp. salt			

Line an 8x4x2-inch loaf pan with foil, extending foil over edges of pan. Butter foil; set aside.

Butter the sides of a heavy 2-quart saucepan. In saucepan combine sugar, evaporated milk, milk, and salt. Cook and stir over medium-high heat to boiling. Carefully clip a candy thermometer to the side of the pan. Cook and stir over medium-low heat to 238°, soft-ball stage (this should take 25 to 35 minutes).

Immediately remove saucepan from heat. Add butter and vanilla, but *do not stir.* Cool, without stirring, to 110°, lukewarm (about 55 minutes). Remove candy thermometer from saucepan. Beat vigorously with a wooden spoon till fudge becomes very thick and just starts to lose its gloss (about 10 minutes total).

Immediately spread fudge into the prepared pan. Score into 1-inch squares while warm. Top each square with a piece of nut, if desired. When candy is firm, use the foil to lift it out of the pan. Cut into squares. Store, tightly covered, in the refrigerator. Makes about 1 pound (32 servings).

Peppermint Creams

Treat this mixture like a sugar-cookie dough, re-rolling and re-cutting scraps and decorating as your fancy dictates.

2½ cups sifted powdered sugar
4 tsp. dried egg whites*
2 Tbsp. water

10 to 12 drops peppermint extract
Paste food coloring (optional)

In a large mixing bowl stir together 1½ cups of the powdered sugar and the dried egg whites. Add water, peppermint extract, and food coloring, if desired. Beat on low speed with an electric mixer till smooth. Gradually add as much of the remaining powdered sugar as you can, beating on low speed till combined. Knead in any remaining powdered sugar. (The mixture should be very stiff and not sticky.)

Divide mixture in half. Wrap one portion in plastic wrap; set aside. Sprinkle a little additional powdered sugar onto a piece of waxed paper. Place the unwrapped portion of the mixture on sugared paper; sprinkle with a little more powdered sugar to prevent sticking. Roll out to ¼-inch thickness. Cut into bite-size shapes with a small cookie or hors d'oeuvre cutter, rerolling scraps as necessary. Line a baking sheet with waxed paper; place candies on paper. Repeat with remaining dough. Cover loosely with a towel and let dry overnight. Store in an airtight container. Makes 1 cup dough (about 60 candies).

*Note: You can find dried egg whites in stores where cake decorating supplies are sold.

Speculaas

Dutch bakers named this crisp cookie from the Latin word for "mirror" (pronounced SPEC-oo-lahs). When they pressed the dough into a wooden mold, the cookie mirrored its shape. We took a little baker's license and used fanciful cookie cutters.

4 cups all-purpose flour
4 tsp. baking powder
1 Tbsp. ground cinnamon
1 tsp. ground ginger
1 tsp. ground nutmeg
1 tsp. ground cloves
½ tsp. salt

1 cup butter
1½ cups sugar
2 eggs
2 tsp. finely shredded lemon peel
2 tsp. finely shredded orange peel
⅓ cup milk
Powdered Sugar Icing (optional, see recipe, page 60)

In a medium mixing bowl stir together flour, baking powder, cinnamon, ginger, nutmeg, cloves, and salt; set aside. In a large mixing bowl beat butter with an electric mixer on medium speed for 30 seconds or till softened. Add sugar and beat about 4 minutes or till fluffy. Add eggs and lemon and orange peels; beat on medium speed till combined. Add about one-third of the flour mixture and beat on low speed till combined. Beat in milk.

Beat in as much of the remaining flour mixture as you can, then use a wooden spoon to stir in any remaining flour mixture. Divide dough into 4 portions. Cover and chill about 1 hour or till easy to handle.

On a lightly floured surface, roll dough, one portion at a time, to ⅛-inch thickness. Using cutters, cut into desired shapes. Arrange cookies 1 inch apart on an ungreased cookie sheet.

Bake in a 350° oven for 8 to 10 minutes or till golden. Cool on a wire rack. Decorate with Powdered Sugar Icing, if desired. For the snowflake design as pictured on pages 56-57, use a fine paintbrush to apply icing. When icing is dry, store in an airtight container. Makes about 65 cookies.

Lebkuchen

The good cooks of Nuremberg, Germany, pulled out all the stops when creating this holiday cookie, adding their cache of candied fruits and almonds to the rich, honey-sweetened dough. The traditional cookies were pressed into large, decorative molds; we've sliced ours into smaller diamonds for ease in storing and snacking.

1	cup honey	2	eggs
1	cup packed brown sugar	½	cup butter, softened
4½	cups all-purpose flour	1	cup diced mixed candied fruits and peels
1	Tbsp. ground cinnamon	1	cup slivered almonds
1	tsp. baking powder		Whole blanched almonds (optional)
1	tsp. ground nutmeg		

In a medium saucepan warm honey and brown sugar over low heat, stirring till dissolved; remove from heat. Set aside to cool.

Meanwhile, stir together flour, cinnamon, baking powder, and nutmeg; set aside. Place honey mixture in a large bowl. With an electric mixer on medium speed, beat in eggs, one at a time, and butter. Add candied fruits and peels and slivered almonds; beat on low speed till combined. Add flour mixture; beat till dough is smooth. Cover and refrigerate overnight.

On a lightly floured surface, roll half the dough at a time to ⅛- to ¼-inch thickness. Cut into 1½-inch diamonds with a knife. If desired, press a whole almond in the center of each diamond. (Or, cut into desired shapes with cookie cutters.) Arrange cookies on a cookie sheet. Bake in a 350° oven for 10 to 12 minutes or till golden. Transfer cookies to a wire rack to cool. Store in an airtight container or in the freezer for 6 weeks. Makes about 96 cookies.

Note: To soften slightly, store cookies with a quartered apple in an airtight container at room temperature for a few days.

Favorite Sugar Cookies

If you have a carton of eggnog in the wings, use a bit to enrich these cookies. Otherwise, milk and vanilla can stand in nicely.

⅓	cup butter	¾	cup sugar
⅓	cup shortening	1	Tbsp. dairy eggnog or milk*
2	cups all-purpose flour	1	tsp. baking powder
1	egg	1	recipe Powdered Sugar Icing (optional)

In a large mixing bowl beat butter and shortening with an electric mixer on medium speed for 30 seconds. Add about half of the flour, the egg, sugar, eggnog or milk, and baking powder. Beat till combined. Beat in remaining flour. Divide dough in half. Cover and chill for 3 hours.

On a lightly floured surface, roll half of the dough at a time to ⅛-inch thickness. Cut into desired shapes with a cookie cutter. Place on an ungreased cookie sheet.

Bake in a 375° oven for 7 to 8 minutes or till edges are firm and bottoms are very light brown. Cool cookies on a wire rack. If desired, frost with Powdered Sugar Icing. Decorate as desired. Store in an airtight container. Can be frozen iced or plain. Makes about 40 cookies.

*Note: If using milk, add 1 teaspoon vanilla.

Powdered Sugar Icing: Combine 2 cups sifted powdered sugar and 2 tablespoons eggnog or milk. Stir in additional eggnog or milk till of drizzling consistency. Tint with food coloring, if desired. Makes 1 cup.

Cranberry Shortbread

Traditionally, these Scottish teatime treats were baked as a large round. The edge was scalloped to resemble the sun's rays (in otherwise short supply in dreary December). Today, many cooks prefer to cut the dough into bite-size cookies.

2½ cups all-purpose flour	1 cup butter
½ cup sugar	½ cup finely snipped dried cranberries*
¼ tsp. salt	

In a mixing bowl stir together flour, sugar, and salt. Cut in butter till mixture resembles fine crumbs. Stir in cranberries. Form into a ball and knead till smooth. Divide into 2 equal portions.

To make wedges, on an extra-large ungreased cookie sheet, pat or roll each dough portion into an 8-inch circle. (If two 8-inch circles don't fit on one baking sheet, use two smaller sheets. Rearrange sheets halfway through baking time.) Using your fingers, press to make a scalloped edge. With a knife, *cut each circle into 16 pie-shaped wedges.* Leave wedges in the circle shape. Bake in a 325° oven for 25 to 30 minutes or till bottom just starts to brown and center is set. Cut circle into wedges again while warm.

To make strips or rounds, on a lightly floured surface, pat or roll half the dough to ½-inch thickness. Using a knife, cut into 24 2x1-inch strips; or, using a 1½-inch round cookie cutter, cut into 24 rounds. Place 1 inch apart on an ungreased cookie sheet. Bake in a 325° oven for 20 to 25 minutes or till bottoms just start to brown. Repeat with remaining dough to make 48 strips or rounds total.

Cool on the cookie sheet for 5 minutes. Remove from cookie sheet; cool on a wire rack. Makes 32 wedges or 48 strips.

*Note: To finely snip cranberries, toss the cranberries in a bowl with 1 tablespoon of the flour. Place cranberries and flour in a blender container. Cover and blend for 30 seconds or till cranberries are finely "snipped."

Vanilla Nut Crescents

Just say "Yes." Vanilla sugar is one of life's little luxuries. It's easy to sanction, for the classy bean can flavor heaps and heaps of sugar.

1 cup butter	1½ cups almonds or hazelnuts (about 6 oz.), ground
½ cup vanilla sugar* or granulated sugar	Colored sugar (optional)
1½ cups all-purpose flour	

In a medium mixing bowl beat butter with an electric mixer on medium speed for 30 seconds. Add vanilla sugar; beat till fluffy. On low speed beat in as much of the flour as you can with the mixer. Using a wooden spoon, stir in ground nuts and remaining flour till combined. Form dough into a ball. If necessary, wrap in plastic wrap and chill about 1 hour or till easy to handle.

Form dough into 1-inch balls, then roll by hand into 2½-inch lengths. Place 1 inch apart on ungreased baking sheets, curving to form crescents. (If desired, sprinkle with colored sugar before baking.)

Bake in a 350° oven for 10 to 12 minutes or till bottoms are slightly golden. Cool on the cookie sheet for 1 minute, then transfer cookies to a wire rack. (Cookies will deflate slightly.) Cool completely. Store in an airtight container. Makes about 50 cookies.

*Note: To make vanilla sugar, split a vanilla bean lengthwise; immerse in a jar with 2 cups granulated sugar. Cover and let stand for 1 week. (Use extra vanilla sugar to replace the sugar in other recipes or in beverages.)

Battenberg Cake

The British Royals trace their roots back to Germany, and so does this cake. It was a favorite of Queen Victoria's daughter, Beatrice, whose married name, Battenberg, became Anglicized to Mountbatten. In this age of "less is more," we've reduced the traditional four layers to three.

1 16-oz. pkg. pound cake mix	2 7-oz. pkg. marzipan
⅛ tsp. red paste food coloring	Sifted powdered sugar
2 Tbsp. orange juice	Sugared Raspberries (optional)*
½ cup seedless red raspberry jam	Sugared Mint Leaves (optional)*
2 Tbsp. light-colored corn syrup	

Grease and flour two 8x4x2-inch loaf pans; set aside. Prepare pound cake mix according to package directions. Spread half of the batter in one of the prepared pans. Stir food coloring thoroughly into remaining batter; spread in the second pan. Bake according to package directions or till cake springs back when lightly touched. Cool in pans on a wire rack for 10 minutes; remove from pans and cool completely.

To assemble, trim crusts from the sides, ends, and top of each pound cake to make evenly shaped loaves. Cut each loaf lengthwise into thirds to make a total of 6 sections. Lay each section on its side and cut each one in half again lengthwise. There should be a total of 12 logs measuring approximately 7½x1x¾ inches. Set aside 2 plain logs and 1 pink log for another use. Assemble cake using 5 pink logs and 4 plain logs.

Drizzle the 9 logs with orange juice; set aside. In a small saucepan combine raspberry jam and corn syrup; heat and stir till jam is melted and mixture is smooth; set aside.

In a bowl, knead marzipan with hands to soften. Sprinkle both sides of marzipan with powdered sugar; roll marzipan between 2 sheets of waxed paper to a 12x8-inch rectangle. (If desired, roll marzipan to an 15x8-inch rectangle; trim off 3 inches from a short side and use this to cut small shapes for garnishes.) Brush off any excess powdered sugar.

Remove top sheet of waxed paper. Place a plain-colored cake log crosswise in the center of marzipan sheet. Brush jam mixture on all sides of cake log. Place pink-colored logs on each side of first log and brush them with more of the jam. For second layer, place another pink log on top of the plain log and plain logs atop the first pink logs, brushing all sides with jam. Repeat layering with remaining cake logs, alternating coloring to make a checkerboard pattern. Press cake logs together.

Bring marzipan up over the sides of cake, having edges meet at the top of the cake, covering the long sides but not the ends. Crimp edges of marzipan to seal; decorate top with marzipan trimmings as desired. Carefully transfer to a serving plate. Using a serrated knife, trim cake and marzipan to make each end even.

Cover and let cake stand for several hours or overnight before serving. Garnish with Sugared Raspberries and Mint Leaves, if desired. Makes 8 to 10 servings.

Sugared Raspberries and Mint Leaves: Place 2 teaspoons dried egg whites (available in cake-decorating stores) and ¼ cup water in a 6-ounce custard cup; stir together with a wire whisk or fork. Place superfine or granulated sugar in a shallow dish. Using a pastry brush, brush egg white mixture onto berries and leaves; roll in sugar. Allow to dry on a wire rack. Arrange atop marzipan frosting.

Rumtopf

Store this fruit topping in a tall, narrow jar or crock to keep most fruit beneath the syrup. Spoon some over ice cream or pound cake when you're ready to celebrate. You may make the rumtopf in summer, as in our story, or in December, using winter fruits.

1½ cups packed brown sugar	4 large pears, cored and cut up
1 cup water	2 cups seedless red grapes, halved (if desired)
4 medium nectarines or peaches (peeled, if peaches), pitted and sliced, or one 16-oz. pkg. frozen unsweetened peach slices, thawed	1 medium pineapple, peeled, cored, and cut up
	2 ½ to 3 cups rum

In a medium saucepan combine brown sugar and water. Cook and stir over medium-low heat till sugar is dissolved. Cool.

In a 4-quart tall, nonmetal crock or jar combine nectarines or peaches, pears, grapes, and pineapple. Pour cooled syrup mixture over fruit.

Add enough rum to cover fruit; stir gently to combine. Store, covered, in a cool place overnight. Place in the refrigerator and store, covered, for up to 4 months, stirring occasionally, using portions as desired*. Let stand at room temperature for 30 minutes before serving. Makes about 3 quarts mixture (24 servings).

Note: To replenish Rumtopf, add 2 cups chopped fruit and ½ cup packed brown sugar to replace every 2 cups of fruit and syrup removed (the top layer may darken). Store in the refrigerator.

Lemon Curd Tarts

A lemon-lover alert: These intensely tangy tarts are more addictive than the proverbial potato chip. Dare you to eat just one!

1¼ cups all-purpose flour	2 tsp. finely shredded lemon peel
⅓ cup granulated sugar	½ cup lemon juice
2 tsp. finely shredded lemon peel	¼ cup water
½ cup cold butter	2 Tbsp. butter
1 beaten egg yolk	3 beaten egg yolks
2 Tbsp. cold water	Powdered sugar (optional)
⅔ cup granulated sugar	Lemon peel curls (optional)
1 Tbsp. cornstarch	

In a medium mixing bowl stir together flour, the ⅓ cup sugar, and the 2 teaspoons lemon peel. Cut in the ½ cup cold butter till mixture is crumbly. In a mixing bowl combine the beaten egg yolk and 2 tablespoons cold water. Gradually stir yolk mixture into flour mixture. Gently knead the dough just till a ball forms. If necessary, cover with plastic wrap and chill for 30 to 60 minutes or till easy to handle.

Meanwhile, prepare lemon curd. In a medium saucepan stir together the ⅔ cup sugar and cornstarch. Stir in the remaining 2 teaspoons lemon peel, lemon juice, ¼ cup water, and the 2 tablespoons butter. Cook and stir over medium heat, uncovered, till thickened and bubbly.

Slowly stir about half the lemon mixture into the 3 beaten egg yolks. Then return all of the egg mixture to the saucepan; stir to combine. Bring to boiling; reduce heat. Cook and stir for 2 minutes more. Transfer to bowl. Cover surface with plastic wrap; chill while pastry shells bake.

For tassies, divide chilled dough into 36 pieces. Press 1 piece onto bottom and up sides of a 1¾-inch tassie pan; repeat with remaining pieces*. Bake in a 375° oven for 8 to 10 minutes or till golden.

(Or, for mini-tart shells, divide chilled dough into 24 pieces. Press 1 piece onto bottom and up sides of a 2¼-inch mini-tart pan; repeat with remaining pieces*. Place pans on a baking sheet; prick with a fork. Bake in a 375° oven for 12 to 14 minutes or till golden.)

Cool in pans on a wire rack; unmold. Spoon a rounded teaspoon of lemon curd into each tassie or a scant tablespoon into each tart; cover with plastic wrap and chill for up to 2 hours before serving. Before serving, decorate with sifted powdered sugar and lemon peel, if desired. Makes 36 tassies or 24 mini tarts.

Note: If necessary, keep part of the dough chilled as you bake the pastries.

Make-ahead directions: Prepare dough as directed. Wrap in plastic wrap and freeze for up to 1 month. Thaw dough in the refrigerator 1 day before working with it. Once baked, the tart shells may be stored in a covered container at room temperature for up to 4 days or frozen for several weeks. Store lemon curd in the refrigerator for up to 1 week.

Holiday Frittata

A time-friendly dish when time matters most. This red-and-green open-faced omelet can rest a few minutes after broiling, for it won't fall or toughen if it needs to wait.

1	Tbsp. cooking oil	⅛	tsp. pepper
1	cup fresh or frozen broccoli florets	10	beaten eggs or 2½ cups refrigerated or
½	large red sweet pepper, seeded, thinly sliced		frozen egg product, thawed
¼	cup chopped onion	2	Tbsp. milk
½	tsp. dried Italian seasoning, crushed	2	Tbsp. finely shredded Parmesan cheese
¼	tsp. salt		Curly endive (optional)

In a 10-inch broilerproof or regular skillet* heat oil over medium heat. Add broccoli, sweet pepper, onion, Italian seasoning, salt, and pepper. Cook and stir till florets are crisp-tender, about 4 minutes for fresh broccoli and 5 minutes for frozen broccoli.

In a medium mixing bowl stir together eggs or egg product and milk. Pour over vegetable mixture. As the eggs begin to set, run a spatula around the edge of the skillet, lifting the egg mixture to allow the uncooked portions to flow underneath. Continue cooking and lifting edges till eggs are nearly set. (The surface will be moist).

Remove skillet from heat; sprinkle with cheese. Broil 4 to 5 inches from the heat for 1 to 2 minutes or till top is just set. (Or, if using a regular skillet, remove skillet from heat. Cover and let stand for 3 to 4 minutes or till set.) To serve, cut into wedges. Garnish with curly endive, if desired. Makes 6 main-dish servings.

Note: Cover the handle of a regular skillet with double thickness of foil to protect it under the broiler.

Minty Winter Compote

Fresh mint, pomegranates, and citrus peel balance the sweetness of the fruit.

1	15½-oz. can pineapple chunks (juice pack)	1	Tbsp. finely slivered orange peel
2	Tbsp. sugar	2	oranges, peeled, halved, and sliced ¼ inch thick
2	Tbsp. snipped fresh mint or 1½ tsp. dried mint, crushed	1	kiwifruit, peeled and sliced ¼ inch thick
1	Tbsp. finely slivered grapefruit peel	¼	cup pomegranate seeds
2	red grapefruit, peeled, halved, and sliced ¼ inch thick		Fresh mint leaves

Drain pineapple, reserving juice; add enough water to pineapple juice to make 1 cup. In a small saucepan combine reserved juice mixture, sugar, and snipped mint. Bring just to boiling; reduce heat. Simmer, covered, for 5 minutes. Strain, discarding mint. Cool slightly.

Meanwhile, in a large bowl combine pineapple, grapefruit peel and slices, orange peel and slices, and kiwifruit; set aside. Pour the strained syrup over fruit; cover and chill for 2 hours or overnight. To serve, stir in pomegranate seeds; garnish with fresh mint. Makes 6 (¾-cup) servings.

Christollen Bread

Germans have baked this rich, fruit-filled bread at Christmastime ever since the Middle Ages. It's particularly tasty toasted.

4¾ to 5¼ cups all-purpose flour
2 pkg. active dry yeast
1 tsp. ground cardamom
1¼ cups milk
½ cup sugar
½ cup butter or margarine
¾ tsp. salt

1 egg
1 cup diced mixed candied fruits and peels
1 cup raisins
¾ cup chopped walnuts
1 Tbsp. finely shredded lemon peel
  Milk

In a large mixing bowl stir together 2 cups of the flour, the yeast, and cardamom. In a medium saucepan heat and stir the milk, sugar, butter or margarine , and salt till warm (120° to 130°) and margarine or butter is almost melted. Add to flour mixture along with egg. Beat with an electric mixer on low speed for 30 seconds, scraping bowl constantly. Beat on high speed for 3 minutes. Using a spoon, stir in candied fruits and peels, raisins, walnuts, and lemon peel; then stir in as much of the remaining flour as you can.

Turn out onto a lightly floured surface. Knead in enough remaining flour to make a moderately soft dough that is smooth and elastic (3 to 5 minutes total). Shape into a ball. Place in a greased bowl; turn once to grease the surface. Cover and let rise in a warm place till double (about 1 to 1½ hours).

Punch dough down. Turn out onto a lightly floured surface. Divide in half; divide each half into thirds. Cover; let rest for 10 minutes. With hands, roll each piece into a 1-inch-thick rope about 15 inches long. Line up 3 of the ropes, 1 inch apart, on a greased baking sheet. Starting in the middle, braid by bringing left rope underneath center rope; lay it down. Then bring right rope under new center rope; lay it down. Repeat to end.

On the other end, braid by bringing outside ropes alternately over center rope to center. (Braid the ropes loosely so the bread has room to expand.) Press rope ends together to seal. Repeat braiding with remaining 3 ropes on another greased baking sheet. Cover and let rise till nearly double (about 1 hour).

Brush loaves with milk. Bake in a 350° oven for 20 to 25 minutes or till golden and loaves sound hollow when tapped. If necessary, cover with foil the last few minutes to prevent overbrowning. Remove from baking sheets. Cool completely on a wire rack. Makes 2 loaves (32 servings).

French Spice Cake

This honey cake traces its roots back to the kitchens of 15th-century France. More like a dense bread than a cake, a slice goes well with a handful of nuts and dried fruits.

1 cup honey
1 cup boiling water
2 tsp. finely shredded
  lemon peel
3½ cups all-purpose flour
1 cup sugar
1 tsp. baking powder

1 tsp. ground cinnamon
½ tsp. baking soda
¼ tsp. salt
¼ tsp. ground cloves
3 beaten eggs
½ cup cooking oil
  Whipped cream (optional)

In a small mixing bowl stir together honey, boiling water, and lemon peel; set aside. In a large mixing bowl stir together flour, sugar, baking powder, cinnamon, baking soda, salt, and cloves. Add the warm honey mixture to flour mixture, stirring with a wooden spoon till nearly smooth. Stir together beaten eggs and oil; add to batter and stir just till combined.

Pour batter into a well-greased and floured 10-inch fluted tube pan. Bake in a 325° oven about 50 minutes or till a toothpick inserted near center comes out clean. Cool in pan on a wire rack for 10 minutes. Remove from pan and cool completely. Wrap and store overnight. Serve with whipped cream, if desired. Makes 18 servings.

Plum Pudding

Fresh plums in December? Not in the olden days. This traditional British Christmas pudding uses dried plums—prunes—instead. If you have a second mold and kettle, you may double the recipe and present one as a gift.

1½ cups pitted prunes, snipped
½ cup brandy or orange juice
1 medium apple, peeled and finely shredded
¾ cup chopped walnuts
½ cup diced mixed candied fruits and peels
1 Tbsp. finely shredded orange peel
3 cups all-purpose flour
1 tsp. ground cinnamon
½ tsp. baking soda

½ tsp. salt
½ tsp. ground ginger
½ tsp. ground nutmeg
1½ cups packed brown sugar
½ cup butter or margarine, softened
3 eggs
1¼ cups milk
1 recipe Hard Sauce (optional)
   (see recipe, below)

In a medium mixing bowl soak prunes in brandy or orange juice, covered, in a cool place for 2 hours or overnight or till most of the liquid is absorbed. Do not drain. Stir shredded apple, walnuts, candied fruits and peels, and orange peel into prune mixture; set aside.

Stir together flour, cinnamon, baking soda, salt, ginger, and nutmeg; set aside.

In a large mixing bowl beat together brown sugar and butter or margarine with an electric mixer on medium speed till combined. Add eggs, one at a time, beating on low speed just till combined (do not overbeat). Add flour mixture alternately with milk, beating on low speed after each addition just till combined. By hand, fold in prune mixture.

Grease and flour a 12-cup fluted tube mold or pan. Spread batter in mold. Lightly grease a square of foil; cover mold with foil, greased side down. Press foil tightly against the rim of mold. Place mold on a rack in a deep kettle containing 1 inch of simmering water. Cover kettle; steam over low heat for 1½ to 2 hours or till a toothpick inserted near center comes out clean, adding additional boiling water if necessary. Remove from kettle. Cool 15 minutes. Carefully invert and and remove pudding from mold. Cool slightly on wire rack. Serve warm with Hard Sauce, if desired. Makes 18 servings.

Make ahead directions: Cool completely and wrap in 100 percent cotton cheesecloth moistened with additional brandy or orange juice. Wrap tightly with foil and store in refrigerator for up to 2 weeks. To reheat, unwrap pudding and remove cheesecloth; return pudding to the mold or pan. Cover tightly with foil and place on a rack in kettle containing 1 inch of simmering water. Cover kettle; steam over low heat for 30 to 40 minutes or till heated through.

Or, unwrap pudding and remove cheesecloth. Place pudding on a microwave-safe plate. Cover with vented plastic wrap. Micro-cook on 50% power (medium) for 6 to 10 minutes or till heated through, turning once.

Hard Sauce

¾ cup butter
1¼ cups sifted powdered sugar

3 Tbsp. brandy, rum, or orange juice
½ tsp. vanilla

In a medium mixing bowl beat together butter and sifted powdered sugar till fluffy. Beat in brandy, rum, or orange juice and vanilla. Store, covered, in refrigerator for up to 2 weeks. Let stand at room temperature for 30 minutes before serving. Makes 1¼ cups.

Mincemeat-Pear Pie

Sign of the times: Most mincemeat no longer contains minced meat and suet. Another modern touch: These days you may purchase prepared mincemeat in jars. Our version pushes the envelope even further by tempering the savory spicy filling with fresh pears. For winter baking, Bosc pears are a good choice.

3 cups thinly sliced, peeled, and cored pears (3 medium)
1 27-oz. jar mincemeat (2⅔ cups)
1 Tbsp. lemon juice

1 15-oz. pkg. folded refrigerated unbaked piecrusts (2 crusts)
Milk (optional)
Coarse sugar (optional)
1 recipe Hard Sauce (optional) (see page 71)

For filling, in a medium mixing bowl stir together pears, mincemeat, and lemon juice. Line a 9-inch pie plate with one of the piecrusts. Transfer filling to pastry-lined pie plate; flute edge. Cover edge of pie with foil. Bake in a 375° oven for 25 minutes; remove foil. Continue baking for 20 to 25 minutes or till pastry is golden. Cool on a wire rack.

Meanwhile, on a lightly floured surface, with a knife or cookie cutter cut remaining piecrust into stars or other decorative shapes. Place cutouts on an ungreased cookie sheet. If desired, brush with milk; sprinkle with coarse sugar. Bake alongside the pie about 10 minutes or till golden. Transfer cutouts to a wire rack; cool. To serve, arrange cutouts atop pie. Serve with Hard Sauce, if desired. Makes 8 servings.

Mincemeat-Pear Tarts: Divide each unbaked piecrust into 4 portions (8 pieces total). Shape 6 portions into balls. Roll out each ball between pieces of waxed paper to 6-inch circles. Ease each into a 4- to 4½-inch tart pan. Flute edges or trim evenly with tart pans.

Divide filling among tart shells (about ¾ cup per tart). With a knife or cookie cutter, cut remaining pie-crust into stars or other decorative shapes. Place cutouts atop tarts. If desired, brush cutouts with milk and sprinkle with sugar.

Bake in a 375° oven for 35 to 40 minutes or till pastry is golden and filling is bubbly.

Makes 6 tarts (12 servings).

Afterword

No story, however short, could be published without the work of a team of people. If you have enjoyed Emma's Christmas Wish, *please join me as I offer my thanks to those who made it possible.*

To Pam Johnson, Hugh Kennedy and Jann Williams at Meredith Custom Publishing, who lovingly edited, designed and oversaw this book. Thank you for your extraordinary professionalism and attention to detail—and for making this experience such a happy one.

To Jean LemMon, Nancy Byal and Joy Taylor at Better Homes and Gardens® *magazine, who dreamed up this project in the first place. Thank you for your enthusiasm and encouragement, and all your good ideas.*

To Cary Phillips, whose beautiful illustrations brought this story alive. Thank you.

To Regula Noetzli, my agent and dear friend. I don't know what I'd do without you in both of those roles.

My thanks must also go to Yvonne Oliger, Mary Seibert and Zoe Kean at the Brown County Public Library, who worked so hard to find me the right material and called me so sweetly when they were overdue! To Dr. Stephen Weber, for his research into what ailed Jan and for making me laugh along the way; to Jamie Andree, Deborah Hutchinson, Steve Kowalski and Pat Richardson for listening to my scribblings and offering such important suggestions; and to Michael Jacobson for his invaluable European research and for that famous red spider... And, finally, to Greg and Charley, my beloved family, who make each day worthwhile.

Merry Christmas to you all!

Sallyann J. Murphey